Sports Stars

ERIC DICKERSON

Record-Breaking Rusher

By Rich Roberts

CHILDRENS PRESS ®
CHICAGO

Cover photograph: Bryan Yablonsky
Inside photographs courtesy of the following:
Vic Milton, pages 6, 9, 36, and 40
George Gojkovich, pages 11, 17, and 23
Ira Golden, pages 13, 15, 24, 29, 33, and 35
Ron Wyatt, page 19
Kevin W. Reece, pages 27 and 42
Ray De Aragon, pages 30 and 38

Library of Congress Cataloging in Publication Data

Roberts, Rich.
　Eric Dickerson: record-breaking rusher.

　(Sport stars)
　Summary: A brief biography of one of the star players of the Los Angeles Rams Football team.
　1. Dickerson, Eric, 1960-　　—Juvenile literature.
2. Football players—United States—Biography—Juvenile literature. [1. Dickerson, Eric, 1960-　. 2. Football players.
3. Afro-American—Biography] I. Title. II. Series.
GV939.D52R62　1985　　796.332'092'4 [B] [92] 85-13234
ISBN 0-516-04349-8

Copyright © 1985 by Regensteiner Publishing Enterprises, Inc.
All rights reserved. Published simultaneously in Canada.
Printed in the United States of America.

1 2 3 4 5 6 7 8 9 10 R 94 93 92 91 90 89 88 87 86 85

Sports Stars

ERIC DICKERSON

Record-Breaking Rusher

Eric Dickerson may be the best ball carrier ever to play football. Even O.J. Simpson thinks so.

"He could be the best there ever was," Simpson said.

Dickerson gained 1,808 yards in his first season in the National Football League in 1983.

That's more than a mile. He gained 2,105 yards the next season to break Simpson's record.

Dickerson plays for the Los Angeles Rams. The Rams' uniforms are easy to spot. They are blue and gold with horns painted on the helmets.

Eric is easy to spot, too. He is No. 29, and on most of the Rams' plays he runs with the football.

Eric is 6 feet, 3 inches tall and weighs 220 pounds. He is big, fast, and tough. When opponents try to tackle him, he can push them away with a straight-arm, dodge them, or run away from them. All of those things make him a great ball carrier.

Eric wears No. 29 for the Los Angeles Rams.

But Eric said when he is running with the football he never thinks about what he's going to do next.

"It's instinct," he said. "You don't go out there and say I'm going to fake this way and go the other way. You might do it, but you don't think about it."

Eric said he was born with his talent.

"I was blessed," he said. "It was God-given talent."

But he isn't a show-off. When he scores a touchdown he doesn't even "spike" the football. He just drops the ball over his shoulder. Then he thanks his teammates for blocking for him.

Eric carries the football well whether the field is wet or dry.

Eric grew up in Sealy, Texas, a small town of about 4,000 people. His mother was only 16 when he was born. She thought she was too young to take care of him. So Eric was raised by his great aunt Viola. He still calls Viola "Mom." The family didn't have much money, but they were very close.

Eric was good in other sports besides football. In track, he won the Texas state high school championships in the 100-meter and 200-meter races. The 100-meters is about as long as a football field.

He also played Little League baseball. His position was center field.

The Rams' quarterback, Vince Ferragamo, has just given the ball to Eric.

"I was a very good hitter and a good fielder," he said. "But baseball was boring."

When he went to high school, basketball was one of his favorite sports.

"When I was a freshman I could dunk," he said. "I played with the varsity when I was a freshman. I made all-district and all-state my sophomore and junior years, but I didn't play my senior year. I just played football.

"Basketball was OK, but I really didn't care for it like I cared for football. It was just fun. Football seemed more natural for me."

Eric first played football with other kids in his neighborhood.

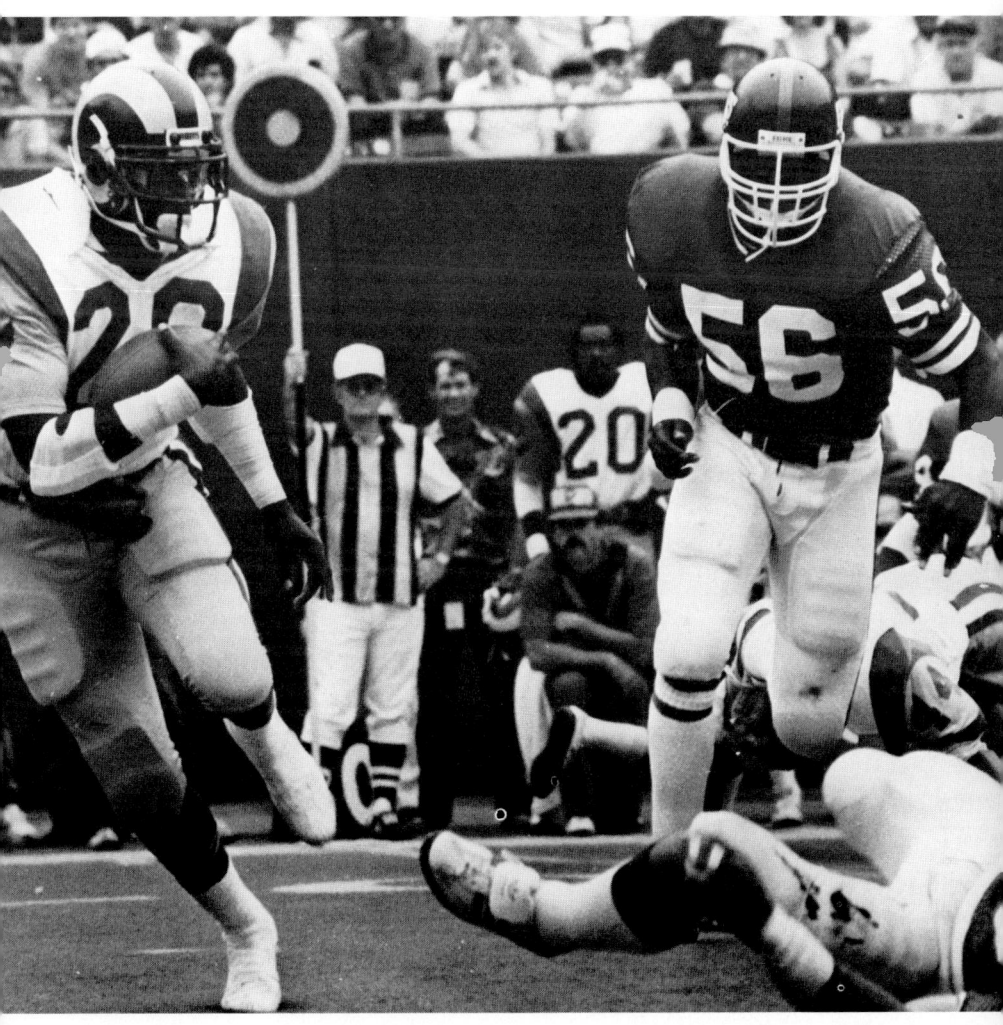

If he wants to keep going, Eric has to avoid No. 56, Lawrence Taylor of the New York Giants.

He said, "When we played football I used to play center all the time because I didn't want to mess up. I never played anything but center for a long time. I was big for my age, but most of the kids were older. I was kind of clumsy. They let me play center and I was satisfied."

Later, when he got to high school, they let him carry the football. In three seasons he gained almost 6,000 yards, and in the state championship game he scored four touchdowns.

After Eric was graduated from high school, many colleges wanted him to come play for them. He decided to go to Southern Methodist University, which is in Texas. Most people call it SMU for short.

Before going to SMU, Eric almost changed his mind and went to the University of Oklahoma. But Viola told him he should go to SMU because he had given the people at SMU his word.

Viola has been a great influence on Eric. Once, when he was unhappy at SMU because he wasn't getting to carry the ball much, he thought about quitting school. She persuaded him to stick it out, and later he was glad he did.

Eric did get to carry the ball. Twice he was honored as the best player in the Southwest Conference.

Eric knows it is important to listen to what other people think and say. While he gets a rest, he and coach John Robinson discuss plays.

After his last season he was third in the Heisman Trophy voting, behind Herschel Walker and John Elway. The Heisman Trophy goes to the best college football player in the country. Many people thought Eric should have won it.

Viola helped Eric make another important decision when he turned pro. The Rams made him their first choice in the National Football League draft, but Eric also was interested in playing for the new United States Football League.

Viola said, "I just told him what I thought was best. I told him that I preferred the Rams because I had heard of them. But it was his decision all the way."

As usual, Eric listened to his "mom." As usual, he was glad he did.

Viola was 80 years old when Eric broke O.J. Simpson's record. She still lives in Sealy but is able to watch all of Eric's games on TV. The Rams' owner, Georgia Frontiere, gave her a satellite dish that can pick up the Rams' games on television from anywhere they play.

Eric lives in California. He is rich and famous, but he still gets homesick. It has been a family tradition to kneel and pray at midnight on New Year's Eve. But when Eric joined the Rams he had to be in Washington D.C. to play a football game on New Year's Eve.

Viola said, "I asked Eric if he got on his knees

at 12 o'clock. He said, 'Mama, you know I did.' "

Eric's younger brother, Leo, lives with him in California, and once or twice during the football season he will buy Viola airplane tickets to come visit him. After the season Eric goes home to Sealy a few times to see his old friends and family.

Eric is very close to his family. During his first season with the Rams he bought gifts for all of his brothers and sisters. He bought a red Cadillac for Viola.

During his second season he had a big house built for Viola near the old one where he grew up. Eric didn't get to see it until he went home after the season.

Eric has given gifts to the players who block for him.

"I love it," he said. "I think I'm going to have a swimming pool put in the back and have it all fenced in. I can see myself putting a lot of time in there."

Eric's best friend is Charles Drayton, who also played football at SMU. Drayton told why Eric does so much for Viola: "Eric wants to give her everything he can while he can," Drayton said. "The bulk of his money is for her to use."

Eric is very appreciative of people who do things for him. After his first season he bought expensive watches for the linemen who blocked for him. After his second season he had special gold and diamond rings made for them, with their names engraved.

Eric said he worries about losing his money foolishly.

He said, "I don't want to read someday where Eric Dickerson, who had a fine eight-year career in the NFL, is bankrupt. I want to read where Eric Dickerson is about to open a $20 million plant."

Eric wants to be a good example for kids. He doesn't drink or smoke and won't have anything to do with drugs.

He said that sometimes he has been at parties where other people were using drugs, but he was never tempted. He said the people respected his beliefs and didn't try to talk him into using drugs.

Eric keeps his body in good shape.

It is a special honor to play in the Pro Bowl game.

He said, "They just said, 'Eric doesn't do drugs,' and that was it. But I don't even like to be around where it's being done. I just get out of there fast."

Some TV people are planning a cartoon series about Eric. He plans to use the series to get his ideas across to kids all over the country.

"I saw the drawings and they looked just like me," he said. "I'll be carrying a message to the kids. I won't be telling them to brush their teeth and wear clean socks, because I didn't want to hear that stuff when I was a kid. It will be more anti-crime, anti-drugs. That kind of stuff."

The kind of stuff Viola taught him.

When Eric was growing up, Viola kept a very strict curfew.

"We had to be in by midnight, even on weekends," Eric said. "One night I stayed out until about 3 A.M., and as I walked up the path to the house I could see someone sitting on the porch. It was her.

" 'Yeah, it's me,' she said. 'Don't you know nothing good happens out at 3 A.M.?' "

Eric was not perfect when he was a kid, but he learned from his mistakes. The principal at Sealy High School was Allen Harwell.

"Eric wasn't a troublemaker," Harwell said.

Brian Kelley of the New York Giants wants to stop Eric from gaining any yards for the Rams.

"But he didn't want to accept everything people told him. He and coach Ralph Harris had some trouble, but they got some things straightened out and he was a real leader after that."

The Los Angeles Rams coach, John Robinson, has said that Eric is fearless when he plays. When he was a rookie with the Rams, opponents tried to frighten him.

Eric said, "In New Orleans, linebacker Rickey Jackson kept saying, 'Every play is going to be tough on you all day.' It was funny. I kept laughing at him."

But Eric was frightened one time. In training before his second season, he was running out

John Robinson, the Los Angeles Rams' coach, cheers on the team.

Eric and his teammates do exercises during warm-up. Eric knows it is important to keep himself in good shape.

for a pass when a teammate ran into him and knocked him down. At first he couldn't get up.

"I was stunned," he said. "My left shoulder and arm went kind of numb. I was scared to move at first. My legs felt weak.

"I prayed a whole lot. I did not want to be paralyzed. If they told me that I couldn't play football anymore but that I could still walk, I'd have said 'fantastic.' I would have hated it, but it would have been OK."

Eric was taken to a hospital.

"It was a freaky thing," he said, "being put on a stretcher and into an ambulance. You always see it happening to other guys. Now it was me.

"I'm grateful. I could be in a wheelchair. You have to go through it to know what it's like. Things like our eyesight and being able to walk, we take for granted."

The accident didn't make Eric afraid to play football. He never was and never will be. Even when he turned pro he wasn't afraid.

"If I went out there feeling like I was afraid, that those other guys were way above my class, I wouldn't play as well," he said.

But he also wears much more protective equipment than most ball carriers. Besides his helmet and shoulder pads, he wears a face mask, mouth-

Eric wears plastic goggles with prescription lenses.

piece, "flak jacket" around his ribs, and extra hip and leg pads.

He also wears plastic goggles with prescription lenses so he can see where he's going. Eric has had to wear glasses since he was in the sixth grade, but that never stopped him from playing any sports.

Most ball carriers think all of that extra gear would slow them down. Eric said he is more concerned about "all them licks," because if he got hurt he wouldn't be able to play.

Eric's teammates also look out for him. After the play is over, they keep other players from hitting him and falling on him. He is a star, but everybody likes him. All the fans want his autograph.

Eric keeps rushing until he is tackled, and gains many yards for the Rams.

Eric is used to it. "I've signed autographs since I was in high school," he said. "I signed 2,000 footballs once."

Tackle Jackie Slater said, "I have an awful lot of respect for Eric. When he came into the league he knew he was going to get a lot of publicity. He could have taken it easy and not worked. But he worked hard every day.

"I consider it an honor to block for Eric. He's something special."

CHRONOLOGY

1960	—Eric Demetric Dickerson is born on September 2 in Sealy, Texas.
1977	—Eric, a junior at Sealy High School, wins Texas state championships in 100-meter and 200-meter events. Eric also wins all-district and all-state honors in basketball and football.
1978	—Eric completes high school football career with 2,653 yards rushing in his senior season, nearly 6,000 for his three-year career.
1979	—Eric enrolls at Southern Methodist University.
1980-82	—Eric breaks Earl Campbell's Southwest Conference records for yards (4,450) and carries (790) and is twice the conference player of the year. He scored 48 touchdowns, including 17 as a senior.
1982	—Eric is voted All-American and is third in the Heisman Trophy voting, behind Herschel Walker and John Elway.
1983 September December	—Eric leads the NFL with 1,808 yards rushing (a record for a rookie), sets a league record with 390 carries, and his honors include: NFL rookie of the year, All-Pro and participation in the Pro Bowl game.
1984	—Eric breaks O.J. Simpson's NFL one-season rushing record with 2,105 yards. Again, he is All-Pro and selected to play in the Pro Bowl.

ABOUT THE AUTHOR

Rich Roberts is a sportswriter for the *Los Angeles Times*. His main assignment is to cover the Rams, which he says gives him the privilege of watching Eric Dickerson play every week.

He has covered six Super Bowl games, writes football articles for various national publications, and is a columnist for *Pro Football Weekly*.

For a change of pace, in the off season Mr. Roberts writes about college basketball, motor sports, golf, and yacht racing.

He is currently on the board of directors of the Professional Football Writers of America.